# Catalyst

Katarina Rivers

Presentation by *BookLeaf Publishing*

Web: www.bookleafpub.com

E-mail: info@bookleafpub.com


ISBN: 9789360948320

First edition 2024

*This book is dedicated to all those who have loved me in a healthy way; those who have encouraged me, supported me, and cheered me on even during the darker stages of my life. I cannot express the gratitude and love I am have for those who have shown me what authentic love is. You are all my heroes.*

# PREFACE

cat·a·lyst

/ˈkadləst/

noun

a substance that increases the rate of a chemical reaction without itself undergoing any permanent chemical change.

"chlorine acts as a catalyst promoting the breakdown of ozone"

a person or thing that precipitates an event.

"the governor's speech acted as a catalyst for debate"

# Overlap

I carry my trauma like a newborn child,
Close to my rapidly beating heart.
I shield it from prying eyes and unwashed hands.
Soothe it when it cries.
Shush it when it screams and shakes.
Sing to it to make it sleep, just for a little bit.
Unlike a newborn though
It is heavy.
And I am tired.
I want to set it down
But I don't know how
Because it howls when I try to leave.
I'm told it makes me stronger
But most days I feel weak.
What people don't see
Is that I am buckling beneath its weight.

It hurts so much to live this way;
To exist in a constant state of distress
To have a lead weight in my chest,
Cotton in my throat.
To bleed and ooze from invisible wounds daily.
They say I survived-
I say I just didn't die.
These are not the same things.

This trauma is immense,
The magnitude is staggering.
I want to share the burden
But it feels like treachery to do so.
I want to throw it into the ocean
And watch it sink down,
Let the salt purify it.
But what if it takes me down with it?
I want to cut it out of me
But I don't know where I stop
And it begins.
It hurts and its too heavy
But who am I without it?
Even I don't know.

# A Noble Heartache

To grieve
Is to have not only have lost something precious
But to have loved something or someone
With every fiber of your being.
To grieve
Is to remember,
To honor,
To hold onto someone
Long after their soul has left this world.
To grieve is to know
That moments are fleeting,
Memories are forever,
And a lifetime is not nearly long enough
To spend with someone whom you adore.
To grieve is the most noble burden.
It is to hold a torch in one hand,
To wipe our eyes with the other,
Carrying on as best we can.
Grief doesn't grow smaller over time-
Instead we grow around it, day by day,
Knowing that torch is still alight
And the love we bare will outlive even
ourselves.

# Gifts

As a mother myself,
I will never be able to understand my own
mother
And the damage she willingly inflicted upon her
children.
I look into the eyes of my children and only
know love-
Even on the long days and even longer nights,
They are everything to me.
The very reason my heart beats, the reason I
breathe.
I cannot imagine screaming cruel words in their
faces daily,
Or choosing men or drugs over them.
They are a part of me forever-
When they were born it felt like a piece of my
soul
Was outside of my body.
I see them and I am so proud of their growth,
I help them correct their mistakes,
Encourage their dreams,
Acknowledge their emotions.
It comes naturally-
I have never once regretted bringing them into
this world.

Instead they are the reasons I push through the
hardest days-
They give me a purpose,
They give me hope.
Their very existence has given me every reason
to do better,
To become better.
The universe knew I needed them before I did.
I was blessed to receive such a tremendous gift
And I'll be damned if I ever squander it.

# Regret

I spent so many years
Stuck inside of my own head-
Self-sabotaging when life seemed to be going
well,
Pushing people away and hiding myself.
I didn't know how to love or be loved.
Because if my own flesh and blood couldn't love
me
How could I ever expect someone else to?

There were so many years I wasted
Wallowing instead of healing.

But those days are gone and they cannot be
changed-
However, that only means I get to wake up every
day now
And choose to push forward-
To heal, to love, to accept love, to create a life I
never dreamed possible.

My only regret in life is that I did not begin
healing sooner.

# Grown

When I was 13 years old
I discovered what it meant to be forged by fire.

Trying to balance my 8th grade school year with
changing diapers, making meals out of very
limited ingredients,
And trying to shield my younger siblings
From the war-zone around us.
I walked on eggshells as I tried my hardest to
keep our heads above water.
Most days I felt like I had cinderblocks tied to
my ankles-
It felt a lot like drowning.

Instead of worrying about school
I worried about eviction notices, EBT benefits
and food scarcity, utilities being turned off, visits
from children's services.

I worried about when the adults around us would
'come down' from their high-
The crashes were unpredictable;
One crash may be seemingly uneventful

But another may result in my mother slitting her
wrists in the kitchen as she screamed how much
she hated me.

That year-
I learned basic first aid, discovered the best
places to hide all the sharp objects and
medications in my house, learned how to pick
the bathroom door lock, and also learned how to
numb myself enough to survive. I learned how
to deescalate people,
It felt like defusing a bomb.

I was only a child myself
But I had to play so many roles-
A mom, a caretaker, a counselor, a mediator, a
punching bag.

That amount of pressure on a child
Changes them in ways you cannot imagine.
I survived off of instant coffee, menthol
cigarettes, and pure spite.
I went to school and isolated myself
Because we never stayed in one place for very
long.
Getting attached was not an option.
I read book after book to have a reprieve and
escape from the hell that was my life.

At age 13, I was a mother to my siblings, to my
niece, and to my own mother.
I was a child but I also wasn't-
I didn't ever have the chance to actually be a kid.
I grew up,
WIld and fearful,
Wise beyond my years.
Wisdom takes a toll on the mind though,
The cost of growing up too fast is
insurmountable at times.

# Dreams

When I was a young child, maybe 3 or 4,
My sister and I would lie in bed, trying to drown
out
The screaming of our mother, the crashing of
thrown dishes
From the other room
We would make up stories
Tiny voices whispering hopes and dreams
Into the smoke drenched air.
All of these dreams
Were simple
A house with hot water,
A kitchen stocked with food,
A dad who wanted to stay,
A mom who didn't lock herself away to get high
Then later came out to berate us for just existing.
At the time,
They all seemed impossible asks-
So they were categorized as fantastical,
Wishful thinking.
I wish I could go back to little-me
And tell her that while we couldn't have that
Growing up,
As an adult we gave it to our children instead
And in doing so,

Those "big dreams" became a reality,
A daily life
Filled with laughter and love,
Singing off key in the kitchen as I cook
pancakes and sip on coffee.
Dancing with my husband
While our children giggle.

I want to hold little-me and tell her
How much better it gets,
She just has to hold on to those dreams.

# Selfish

I used to climb onto the roof outside of my old
bedroom window,
I was terrified of heights (I still am)
But it was one of the few places
I felt untouchable.
I could disappear for a brief time
And no one came looking for me.
It was a place I could cry,
A place I could catch my breath,
Gather my thoughts and put the mask back on-
So I could fight to survive another day.
The fear of heights was absolutely nothing
Compared to the knowledge that if I
Slipped up, got snippy or 'rude' with my mother
or her various boyfriends
I would be spitting blood and chipped tooth
enamel for weeks.
Falling to the ground seemed tempting-
Because either I died and the battle was over
Or at the very least I could stay in the hospital
For a month or longer, if I was lucky.
I would step to the ledge and imagine the ground
rushing up to meet me,
Imagine the impact,
Bones cracking.

But everytime I would remind myself
That if I disappeared
Who would change all of the diapers,
Make the babies their bottles,
Fill the sippy cups, give the kids baths,
Who would fix their food?
Or read them a bedtime story or sing a lullaby to
help my brothers fall asleep?
Who would kiss the boo-boos, would remind
them to brush their teeth?
Who would mediate the arguments between my
mother and sister?
Who would bury the knives under the porch?
Who would flush the pills
And throw out the razor blades?
Who would clean up the blood?
Who would stand between my brothers and the
monsters around us?

Death seemed like a sweet reprieve most of the
time
But it also felt like a selfish luxury
That would only ever hurt
Those I loved most

And so I stayed.

# Family Tree

Growing up
Family was complicated
I cannot even count how many biological fathers
My mother claimed I had.
One dead, one in another state, one in prison,
and various scattered throughout the backroads.
I had family on my mother's side-
Grandparents, an aunt, an uncle, cousins, etc.
But she would only let them see me
On her terms and only when she needed
something-
A gallon of milk, childcare, money, a place to
stay, etc.
I was a pawn and she the queen,
She would hack away at any relationships that
didn't serve her,
No matter if the person loved me and wanted
me.
It was only ever important that she had total
control,
She'd chop the branches off
Of any part of the family tree
That she didn't want,
She ignored the decaying roots,
The diseased bark,
And the crying child at the stump.

# The Healer

He loved me
When I still tasted of heartache and war.
I couldn't quite understand
How anyone could love such a broken thing
And so I pushed him away out of fear-
Fear that one day he would realize
How much work it was to love me,
Fear that ultimately he would leave
Like everyone else in my life had done.
Fear that I wasn't deserving,
Fear that I would destroy him alongside myself.
But he held on with white knuckles
Desperately and devotedly.
He didn't let go
But instead gently held me
And told me of his own wounds
So I felt comfortable sharing my own,
These ugly things I had hidden away for so long
Didn't seem so daunting when his gaze fell upon
them.
He kissed the wounds,
His love was a salve,
His words the anaesthetic.
His love felt like healing,
His heart felt like home.

When I was too lost to face the pain,
He faced it for me,
Always gentle
And encouraged me to
Find beauty among the rubble,
To pick up the pieces of my former self,
And rebuild myself
While he gaze on adoringly
And proudly.
Telling me
"I knew you could it,
I knew you were worth the wait."

# Book Worm

Growing up
I was a voracious reader.
Especially during high school.
I would read at least one book a day,
The school librarians adored me
And let me take out as many books as I wanted.
They thought I was just a vivid reader
And they were more than happy to help foster
my love of literature.

In reality I read to escape-
I didn't want to face my trauma
Or acknowledge the storms brewing in my life.
If I engrossed myself in a fantasty world
I didn't need to deal with the complex emotions
Of being a child, steeped in trauma,
Separated from my siblings,
Living in strangers' homes,
Knowing nothing in my life was permanent.
Chaos was only one step away.

Now as an adult
I sometimes feel ashamed for not reading
As much as I used to.

I try to read a couple chapters each day during
my breaks at work
Because there's rarely a quiet moment when I
am home.

That is a beautiful thing though-
I don't have a life I want to escape from any
more.
Instead I live in the moment
And I find joy all around me,
In my husband and children,
Our dogs,
In my artwork and writing,
In friends and chosen family.

But I will forever be grateful for the books that
saved my life.

# Accountability

I have not always been a good person,
I know this.
I have hurt people needlessly,
I have broken the heart of someone who loved
me.
I have been cruel and judgemental,
I have lived baring my teeth,
White knuckling everything,
I left my claw marks on everything I'd ever held
on to.

Trauma has a way of distorting things-
It left me in wreckage,
All jagged edges-
Anyone who tried to reach for me
Wound up bleeding.
The unhealed parts of me
Had me hurt others.

This is not to excuse to my behavior
Only to explain it.

It took me so many years to do the work
To find myself,

To separate myself from my trauma, from my
past.
To find ways to communicate in a healthy way,
To own up to my actions
To find inner peace
And to let go of the rage inside me.

To those I have harmed,
I am sorry.
You didn't deserve the pain I inflicted upon you.
I do not expect forgiveness or understanding,
This apology is not for me,
Its for you.

I hope you find love and happiness,
I hope you heal as well.

# Side B

Red light kisses,
Eyelash wishes.
Your backseat became a confessional
Where we told each other of all the hurts in our
life
And all the joys.
Shared our dreams and hopes,
Preaching our love like a sermon.

You loved me
Fiercely.
Vibrant with your adoration,
Never ashamed to shout your love
From the rooftops.

My name sounded like a prayer coming from
your lips,
Something holy and beautiful,
Words I could never imagine
Anyone would ever associate with me.

I will forever be grateful for you,
For showing me how to stand on my own
And how to fight for myself.

# Bloodletting

Telling my story
Is my version of
Bloodletting.

An ancient practice,
Often misunderstood
And demonized in modern times.

For me,
It is cathartic.
It brings a sense of healing-

Its like sucking the poison out,
Finally being able to breathe after drowning.

I finally have a voice
And I will never be silent again.

That silence almost destroyed me once,
Never again.

# Aposematism

I've finally left the town
That almost broke me.

Growing up in the bible belt
When you're a mess of a girl
Is not for the faint of heart.

I was hurting
But the only thing the adults around me cared
about
Was whether or not I went to church,
My hair color, my tattoos, and piercings,
The way I dressed,
The music I connected with,
The books I read.

They never asked why,
If they had
I would tell them-

Being 'frightening' looking was my only
defense,
A tough outer shell,
An off putting appearance
Keeps predators away-
Most of the time at least.

# To Love An Addict

To love an addict
Is to wait on that phone call or for your doorbell
to ring-
The one where someone tells you they have
overdosed.

It is to hope
Against all hope
That this time, sobriety sticks,
That the finally break free their disease.

It's 3AM phone calls
Where they are threatening to give up on life.
It's calling local police precincts, hospitals, and
the morgue
When they haven't responded to any calls or
texts in 24 hours.

It's walking on egg shells,
Sitting on pins and needles.
Never knowing what will come next,
The only consistent thing is inconsistency and
chaos.

It's crying in the shower

From relief when they're okay,
Anger that they let you down again,
And sadness because for once, you wish you
were as important to them
As the drugs are.

To love an addict
Is to love a storm of a person-
They are unpredictable and messy,
Downright terrifying at times,
But they are also strikingly beautiful
In only the way that disasters can be.

# Fawn

I'd read about the fight or flight response to an
external threat
And never perfectly fit in one or the other
entirely.
I can fight but prefer not to,
I can run but have never ran far enough to
escape.
I felt like an outsider reading about these
common trauma responses.

Then one day I discovered the 'fawn' response-
And something just clicked inside of me.


I have broken bread with a man who raped me,
Cleaned his home, did his laundry, smiled and
said 'yes sir'.
I apologized to an ex-boyfriend after he sent out
nude photos of me.
I defended my own mother's abuse of me for
years
And played the dutiful role of an adoring
daughter.
I shed a tear for a different man who raped me
when he was murdered,

And another for his mother and another for his
child.

I don't have it in me to be hateful,
I have always worn my heart on my sleeve,
As my great-grandmother would say.

But bigger than that,
If I make myself smaller
I am a less visible target.
If I make myself 'helpful' and obedient,
Then maybe I will be safe.
If I am valuable
Then maybe they won't want to hurt me.

There is safety in submission.

# Reciprocity

I have always tried to love people
The way I want to be loved-
Unconditionally and without ulterior motives.
Unfortunately I have learned the hard way
That some people will only love you
For as long as you can offer them something-
Money, childcare, food,
They will want you to be their free therapist.
These are the people who will
Ask you to set yourself on fire
To keep them warm.
They expect you to cross oceans for them
But they can't even cross puddles for you.
They will take and take and take
Then be angry when you have nothing left to
give.
I want you to know-
These are not your people,
They are not your tribe.
They are blips on your radar,
Wish them well,
Say farewell.
You cannot change them
Nor can you fix their brokenness.
And no amount of words you speak

Will make them see your worth.

Grieve your loss
But don't settle in it.
Instead look for the people
Who light up when you walk in a room,
The ones who build you up,
Who offer you the same love
You have spent years pouring into
those who were ungrateful and took you for
granted.
And when you find these beautiful people
I want you to love them
Just as hard as they love you.

# Disillusioned

Growing up in foster care
Was both a blessing and a curse.
Had I stayed with my origin family
I would not have survived.

But living in a stranger's home
While they constantly reminded me
I didn't belong and
Having them threaten to "send me back"
For minor offenses (like loading a dishwasher
too loudly.)
Did no favors to my already fragile psyche.

Home was not safe,
But the outside world wasn't either.
I was under no illusion
That these families were anything but
placeholders to me
And I, a paycheck to them.

# The Closest

When I was 14 years old
And living at a state run home for foster youths
I was baptised at the local church.

I don't think I knew then what that meant-
I wasn't even sure if I believed in God
Or if I was just clinging to some hope that
Someone was watching over me.

What I did know was the love I was shown
On the day of my baptism.

The pastor would call each child's name
And have them walk to the baptism pool,
Clad in a white robe.
He would then ask that the family stand to
witness this beautiful moment.
When he called my name
I knew that my only blood relative in the
audience
Was my younger brother Curtis.
I was embarassed because I knew only having
one person stand for me
While tons stood for the other kids
Would single me out.

But a beautiful thing happened when the pastor
called out for family to rise:
Every single foster youth stood with smiles,
Every staff member from my group home rose
too.

And as the pastor lowered me into the popl,
I felt this tugging on my heartstrings
As holy water mixed with the saltwater of my
tears,
I felt loved,
I felt seen.

I think that was the closest to God I have ever
felt.

# Catalyst

Every single moment of my life-
The beautiful ones,
The awful ones I thought would decimate me-
They all brought me here,
They paved the way for
The life I have now.

Every single thing in my life
Led me to my present.
They all shaped me in one way or another,
Some for the better,
Some not.

I am unsure who I would have become without
these experiences.
Even the heartbreaking ones have taught me a
lesson or two,
And have helped mold me into who I am now.

Every part of life has served a purpose,
Every one is part of the chain reaction.

www.ingramcontent.com/pod-product-compliance
Lightning Source LLC
LaVergne TN
LVHW010933200726
843509LV00013B/2205

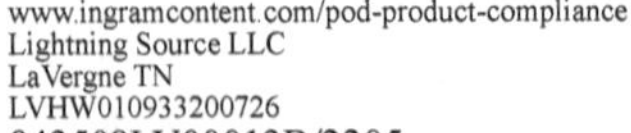